Driving
through
Paintings

Driving
through
Paintings

poems by
Leslie Klein

Shanti Arts Publishing
Brunswick, Maine

Driving through Paintings

Published by Shanti Arts
Interior and cover designed by Shanti Arts

[Cover and pages 10–11] Eagle Lake, from Mountain
Road, Bar Harbor, Maine, c. 1930–1945. Linen texture
postcard. 5.5 x 3.5 inches. Boston Public Library,
The Tichenor Brothers Collection. Public Domain.

[Page One] Brattleboro, Vermont, c. 1930–1945.
Linen texture postcard. 5.5 x 3.5 inches. Boston
Public Library, The Tichenor Brothers Collection.
Public Domain.

Shanti Arts LLC
193 Hillside Road
Brunswick, Maine 04011
shantiarts.com

Printed in the United States of America

ISBN: 978-1-951651-34-3 (softcover)
Library of Congress Control Number: 2020939499

for Scott

and
for my mother,
who would have loved the ride

Contents

ACKNOWLEDGMENTS

Grateful acknowledgment is made to the editors of the following publications where these poems were initially published:

Treasured Poems of America, Sparrowgrass Poetry Forum, Sistersville, West Virginia, 1992: "Letter"

Berkshire Record, Great Barrington, Massachusetts, 2019: "Magic"

Special thanks to Bill and Liza Bennett for their knowledge, encouragement and friendship.

PROLOGUE

Within these pages
the pulse of my life resides.

The journeys taken
ideas birthed
sorrows unveiled.

Within these pages
are expressions
of love—spoken and unsaid.

Here lie the glories of nature—
bird songs and pastures
rivers and shore
births and deaths
felt with the faintest heart.
Enjoyed in the spirit
of the moment.
Remembered reverently
in color, texture and light.

Within these pages
are the little girl I once was
the young woman longing for love
the teacher wishing to inspire
the artist struggling with word and form
the explorer seeking moments
never to be forgotten.

Here lie the threaded stories
that have taken me places that are mine
with insights discovered along the way.

LETTER

An artist captures the absolute
in his hands
stroking its color on canvas.

A musician transforms energy
into tones harmonious to existence.

A dancer moves the unmanifest
through her limbs
in expression of life.

You are an artist yourself—
composing your world
from the impulses received from within.
By expressing your true nature
you are stroking your brush on creation.

That is art.
We are all artists—
casting spells here and there
leaving a part of ourselves
somewhere
as a sculptor marks a stone.

DRIVING THROUGH PAINTINGS

Driving through paintings
of ribbon roads
and jasper fields.
Of red barns
with green silage.

Paintings of pink sunsets
and orange pumpkin patches,
stroking garden plots
with color.

Driving through paintings
of osprey, hawk,
dove and kestrel
soaring over pastures of cows—
black and white on the landscape.

Paintings of bison
breathing white smoke in wintry air.
Bounding over hills in flowing formation,
like starlings swirl in unison through sky.

Driving through paintings
of covered bridges and fishermen
angling on riverbeds in deep boots.

Paintings of sea coves
with placid ocean at low tide.
Woodland paths of pine cover
and sun splashed pond,
where lily pads float serenely—
floral passengers in tow.

Driving through paintings
of steep mountain roads
with red autumn color
curving sharply toward rivers far below—
waterfalls foaming white.

Paintings of small towns
with Victorian houses,
where the smell of morning coffee resides.

Driving through paintings
of apple orchards,
with gracefully shaped trees.
Of crooked fence posts
and arching elms.

Paintings of mountain backdrops
and lattice bridges.
Slivers of lake
reflecting sunlight.

Driving through paintings
of hay bales
patterned on pastures.
Rotund giants of food
for the sweet-faced ewes
and brown-eyed Guernseys.

Paintings of men on tractors,
bare-chested and suntanned,
harvesting corn
from the lush, vast fields.

My Man of the Earth

He is of the earth—
feet planted
in the soil of his beginnings.
Brought to nature's wonder
of brooks and fishing
mountains and deer trails
cows and heifers
barn cats and Princey.

Far from city life
flourishing
in nature's arms
he could forget
sorrows revealed
after coming to this beautiful place.

My man of the earth
crafts the land
with an eye
for the shrub to be saved,
trillium to be nourished,
weed to be pulled
to redefine this sacred space—
created delightedly
forging along the green paths
he has nurtured
and nipped at
so diligently.

This man of the earth
is sweet and gentle
strong and wise.
He drives me
through mountain passes,

along golden fields
and lake vistas.
He brings flowers
for no reason.
Leads me to wild plants
discovered
on wooded paths
at brook's edge.

My man of the earth
walks tall—
head brushing
foliage in high trees.
Lifeless branches
are pruned
on his amble
through leafy domain,
noting the fruit
and small blooms
that accompany each plant.
Remembering their place
to safeguard
and encourage
their growth.

He is of the earth.

MY YOGA KITTY

My yoga kitty
lies on his back
in *shevasanah*
arms and legs relaxed
white, fluffy tummy revealed
rhythmically breathing in yoga fashion—
letting go.

My yoga kitty
lengthens his body
on the floor
arms reaching fully
up and away
from outstretched legs.

My yoga kitty
reaches one soft paw toward me
as I too repose in *shevasanah*.
His head tilts
keeping an eye on my movement
wanting to be close
as he follows my postures.

My yoga kitty
gets up slowly
arching his body
while I alternate in cat and dog pose.
He curves in and out of my arms
touching me lightly with his tail
settling beside my undulating body
as I move from cat to dog
smoothly and rhythmically.

My yoga kitty
purrs deeply
while I breathe in
and out
in my own vibrational hum.

On that Day

We awoke that morning
to the clearest sky—
sun illuminated
on deep, sapphire waters
of Lake Champlain.

Sitting on the porch of our rented cottage
we delighted in the kingfisher's diving antics,
blue heron's slow motion steps,
emerald-headed drake gliding—
the smells and sounds
of first light.

Sipping coffee in this paradise,
beaming at each other,
exultant,
on this shining new day.

"I am so happy."
"Life is so good," we whisper
in our reverie.
Witnessing our world
of picture perfect calm.

Soon our peace
would collapse
as we learn about
the planes heaving
destruction at our towers.
Wreaking an inferno of
death and shock
to the unsuspecting city.

How could it be
that at the same moment
we were blissfully
in peace and optimism,
this dreadful death
landed on our shores?

Life imposes unanswerable questions.
For how many infants were born into love?
How many lovers enthralled,
painters inspired,
dancers soaring,
at the same instant,
as we were,
suspended in a gleaming joy
on that day?

A New Day

As the birds awake
to sing in concert this morning
the nocturnal journey
of the barred owl
with their young
is setting.

Both choruses intermingle—
the pulsing hoots
like the rhythm drum
play a steady beat
as the rise and fall
of the songbird's harmonic flourishes
set the morning melody in place.

The edge of day and night
resound with music
even with the sky still dark
and the moon's light
diminished.

GIVING THANKS

"Leo, she's only a baby!"
my grandmother cried out
to her son, whose hand
was raised to spank me.

I had burned our rug.
Leaving two ashen marks
on its white nap.
Grandma saved me
with those words.
Dad dropped his hand
acknowledging my innocence and age.

For it was his golden cigarette lighter
that called to me that day.
A magical totem
that I watched him fondle,
creating a flame—blue and orange—
to light his smoke.

I had my chance to
investigate this Thanksgiving.
Mom was holed up in the kitchen
chopping, mixing, baking.
I was alone.

As I probed this golden treasure
the light suddenly flickered brightly.
My young mind and hands
did not understand how to extinguish
the flame
before it dropped to the shag.

My naïve logic didn't realize
that the tissues I ran for
would not put out the blaze.
Instead they burst forth
in their own fire,
floating down to the floor.

It is a wonder I wasn't burned.
It is a wonder I didn't make a sound
to distract my mother from her cooking labors.

Somehow, the fire died
and I guiltily schemed a cover up.
Pillows gathered from the bedroom
were placed atop the black scars.
I sprawled upon them
after switching on the television
to innocently watch Howdy Doody.

I vowed to remain on this spot
all night.
Even when grandma, dad, and my uncles arrived
I was frozen.
As dinnertime approached
I was called to the table.
The requests went unheeded,
as I feigned interest
in Clarabelle and Princess Summerfall Winterspring.

They could wait no longer.
It was time to eat.
My frustrated father
reached down for my hand
pulling me up from my lair.

I stiffened as he picked up the pillows
and . . .
Gasps and shrieks filled the room.

I was numb.
All was a blur.
I could not speak.
Dad raised his hand.
But grandma's voice
admonishing her son
cracked my stoic silence.
I cried.
Yet I was saved
on that day of thanksgiving.

SPRING TRAVELER

Felix has arrived
all dapper and fit
from his Costa Rican journey.
He is back home
in our yard
ready to turn on
the charm
to attract a mate.

His long beautiful trill
and Zoro-like mask
so distinct
as he peeks from behind
the leafy boughs
nibbling dried rosehips
and sipping apple blossom nectar.

Good mornings on the rosebush
at our window
are brief
as his concentration
is focused on his gal
who will fastidiously fashion
the nest for their progeny.
More visits will come
when the missus is nesting.

He is a breezy presence
at our breakfast table
speaking to us expectantly
at the window
where we sit with
brimming cups and toast
admiring our young sprite

of a common yellowthroat
as he lives
this chapter of his journey
in the northern climes
creating life in our backyard.

Morning in the Pentagoet

Daybreak stretches goldenrose light
through the turret windows
painting our room with the sun.

The deep blue waterfront
and peninsula across Penobscot Bay
inspires from this third floor perch.

We love this spot—
views in the round
of this sweet, small town of Castine.

Footsteps, clanging cups, spoons, aromas
beckon at 7:00 A.M.
outside our door
where a sideboard
holds morning coffee.

With cups carried inside
to the expanse of windows
we scan the town pulse
from our castle tower—
sipping, savoring.

Main Street falls steeply
down to the harbor,
beyond the corner store,
where locals gather
for their morning brews.

Cadets in starchly pressed uniforms
march through town in pairs,
greeting those they pass
like regimented gentlemen.

This regal Queen Anne Victorian
that houses us
is warm and solid.
We feel very much at home—
sleeping the most peaceful, deep sleep,
dining on delicious fare.
Evenings we stroll along
the narrow seaside roads
admiring the ancient elms
living throughout the town,
resplendent in their green bonnets.

Cared for passionately—
all three hundred of them
numbered, watched, and babied,
as they live what life may be left
before succumbing to Dutch elm disease.
We scrutinize them each year,
performing our own visual health check.
So happy when we see them
full, alive, and thriving.
Though, sadly, we have witnessed
the demise of some giants
as the years turn, and the disease
gets the best of them.

Ding, dong, ding, dong,
on the hour,
the church tower clock chimes.
This melodic tune heard at 2:00 A.M.
is a reassuring lullaby.

Yet, at morning light
the smell of coffee at our door
starts the day luxuriously—
lounging above the town
watching it thrive,
planning our journey
for the day.

GUITAR

Graceful tones of
guitar strings
soar over the room
immersing me in
the dance of sound.

Happily, fingers
glide over notes
urging melody from the
wound sinews
that embrace the
wooden hollow.

This music created
in the realm of angels,
birdsong,
brooks rippling over soft stones,
moth wings aflutter,
humming bees at the nectar.

Quiet Visit

The Japanese couple
spoke to each other
in hushed,
private conversation
as they thoughtfully
analyzed all they
were seeing.
They looped around
the showroom again,
again, and again,
in contemplation,
as the decision
became clearer
for the purchase
they will transport home
representing their American journey.

In their quiet, shy manner
they listened to information
about the clocks
that intrigued,
never saying a word.
The horse
or the teapot
was the dilemma.
They chatted,
faintly,
moving from one to the other
over, and over again,
then walked out of the shop.

Within the hour
they returned
for the teapot,

communicating in short
simple responses
as their treasure
was packed
for its flight.
With a bow and smile
the door closed behind.

TREES

If trees could speak
they would tell tales
of history, family,
love, life, death.

They would mark anniversaries
divulge legends of
kisses under their boughs
in the moonlight.

Speak of kittens
stranded on high branches.
Cries of mothers witnessing
the hanging of a son.

They would reveal scars
from lightening strikes.
Recall pain from a heart carved
with love.

Chat about woodpecker holes,
butterfly chrysalis'
dangling from branches,
overlooking once grassy trails
now transporting
intruding vehicles.

If trees could speak
they would impart a wisdom
cultivated by the years.
An understanding
of the cycles of life
ever in flux,
hard to capture
to retain the pureness
of their beginning.

DESOLATION

Our neighbors
raped their forested land
to a barren ground
dotted with severed
tree stumps and the
promise of
erosion in the
pristine brook
meandering their terrain
to property below
this gash on the landscape.

On its way down a pond filled with silt.
A dam of muck and twig formed in another
while bird, deer, coyote, owl, turkey,
squirrel, chipmunk, bobcat, bear
and other fugitives of this desolate property
left homes
inhabited for decades.

GERMINATION

Just as we behold
sprouting leaves
in our garden,
we witness the cultivation
of our lives.

Observe the nourishing
of our soul,
with people,
with work,
with love,
and our creations.

We know that as we grow,
like the flower,
the tree,
the vine,
we progress.

Moving a little further
toward a goal,
an ending,
an idea,
through a phase.

As the sunlight feeds
the earth,
the light of our ideas,
desires,
even illumination of defeats,
gives us energy
to grow,
to enrich,
to change.

When we stop reaching
for the spark
of imagination and passion,
we die.
As the sun's retreat
devastates the bloom.

Lipstick Smile

Grandma let me wear
her blood red lipstick
to wave to my mother
at her hospital window.

I was seven years old.
Mom had just given birth
to my new brother.
I couldn't see him yet,
for he was in the hospital too.

I was to spend a few days
with my Grandma
helping her bake bread,
make potato pancakes,
watch her knit,
and gaze at wrestling on TV—
her favorite was Haystack Calhoun.

Sitting at her tiny kitchen table
with bread dough braided,
ready for the oven,
I could peer out the window
toward the alley below.
Colorful clotheslines crisscrossed
on their sixth floor journey down.
Shirts blew in the breeze.
I blushed at the underwear
neatly pinned to the line
dancing in the wind,
as if someone was wearing them.

Grandma roasted chicken every week.
The foyer of her apartment
had wishbones strung on cord
near the ceiling
embellishing the molding
that streamed around the walls.
It was an unusual sight,
but grandma thought it was good luck.
When she came to visit
she would always bring one for me
and later, my new brother.

Her knitting bag
was carried everywhere—
needles protruding,
stabbed into skeins
of colorful yarn.
She made lovely shawls
I still wear.

On this special morning
preparing for the hospital visit
I saw her lipstick
in a heavy, gold case
with mirror attached.
I removed its cover,
turning the bottom
to reveal a large red crayon rising.
It tempted me as I gazed
at my pale young lips in the mirror.

I drew the color over my mouth
smiling at my matured,
womanly appearance.
Mom would definitely see me
with these bright lips.
Grandma called for me to hurry.
I bravely left the bathroom
eager for her approval.
She understood.

As I stood on the sidewalk, later,
waving to my beautiful mother
my deep crimson smile
was a vibrant testament
to the love and longing
I felt for her.

BIRD PARADISE

The oriole's flute song
entwines the trees.
Even at their lofty heights
the tones climb and swirl
into the morning rise.

Hopping on green grass,
listening for the worm's crawl
below the sod,
our robin mother
tilts her head to
follow its path.

Later, she flies atop the evergreen
to the precarious limb
to fashion her nursery
with grasses and mud.
She soars back and forth
from the brook's edge
collecting bedding
for the sky blue eggs
that will birth her fledglings.

The black-masked common yellowthroat
is acrobatic on the rose bush
dangling from the dried hips and buds
from last year's blooming.
He is silent from his usual melodic tune,
now, that he has found a mate.

We are grieving for the wood thrush
found on the road.
Our lament is for one less
glorious concert we will hear
from this vocalist,
as the sun lays down.

So happy, when we see another
skipping along the garden path.

THE WRITER

In the dim corners of the room
she dwells
with her fountain pen and parchment.
Pondering a daily miracle
as a sleuth sights a clue
unseen by the naked eye.

This is where
she spends her days
exposing the deepest pain
hidden below the surface.

How could anyone know
that this person—shiny and bright
would be harboring a deep
longing and sadness in life.
Yet, as she recorded the words
on the page,
emotion was liberated.

Only years later
after she is gone
does the message begin to seep
into the reader's mind—
her thoughts considered
jewels of insight.

This is her legacy.
The world now understands
how living in the dark
corners exposed such a
light into the human soul.
Her fragility understood
only in retrospect

after the veil was raised
illuminating the
deep places held within.
Her memory shines
for all who have known
similar longings and disappointment.
Her voice eternal.

FRAGILITY

The blast of
impact on the glass
shattered our
morning peace.
I couldn't look!
He ran outside
finding the victim
fallen
from this brutal thud.

Moments later with small
fox sparrow in hand, he declares,
"I think she'll live!"
Stroking head and wing
rhythmically to sustain consciousness
bathing its tiny body with soothing
warm breath.

This delicate rust-colored
bird crouches safely
in the palm of his hand—
a comfort in the sparrow's fright.

Walking to the
honeysuckle he
places her carefully
so feet
clench a thin branch
holding her upright.

Wobbly and silent,
her eyes meet
the rescuer—whispering encouragement,
while emerging from the injured
cloud.

With every gentle stroke along
head to tail feathers
balance and strength are
regained.

Suddenly in a burst of
reddish wing she flies
magnificently pushing upward
to giant evergreens.

Survival is a constant
thread of life endured
for the most fragile.

He has survived his own
blast of impact
against the steering wheel
of his car, years earlier
in a similar
split second event
that thrust this
bird at our window.

LIBRARY

The library
evokes memories of
musty, private places
where we glimpse other worlds
learning history, science and lore.

Tucked between two shelves
a soft chair awaits.
Cozy, comfy, calm,
yet, pulsing with people
all respectfully guarding
solitude, silence,
and space.

A child's exuberant voice
fills the still room
with shrieks of excitement
for a colorfully,
illustrated book.
Long shushes are heard now
admonishing the little one
about stillness
in this sacred place.

The air smells
of aging pages
and vintage inks.
Threadbare covers
convey the history
of a book's existence
having been touched
by loving hands
throughout its long life.

All the eyes that have
looked at these pages.
All the fingers
that have smoothed
its inked surface,
bringing life
to the imagination,
knowledge to the mind;
breathing love
from sultry stories
into someone's eager heart.

These temples
of wisdom and beauty
still inspire;
thoughtfully constructed
to imbue this sense of sanctuary.
A glorious presence
on the landscape
of our towns.

WILD PAGES

Another book
has come my way
after abandoning
the read of two others
unable to attach
my interest
for more than mere pages.

This one that
ensnares
is riveting
with passion, flora
and carnivore scat.

Enchanting is my
imagined sketch
of backwood events.
All is pulsing—
moths, bats
and milk-gorged teats
consume
as do the kisses
and long stares
of the lovers
entwined in their
discovery.

ANCIENT VISIONS

Ancient artifacts
placed on altars and
adorning walls
are primitive
reminders of when
tool, message and tribute
were refined by hand.

Clay lifted from riverbanks
color from crushed stone or berry
message and imagery incised
with twig or bone.

These expressions
created with heft and brawn
are imbued forever
with the presence of their makers.

I too mingle clay
and tribute
into visions
of my own history.

Unearthed in a distant era
these days will be
relics of time—
my artifacts ancient.

FIRING

The kiln is loaded.
All the new pieces
sit on shelves held aloft by stilts.
It is a mystery as each form changes
while exposed to intense heat.
They shrink and crawl ever so slightly
as the hours fade toward the firing's end—
transformed to a hardened beauty.

As the timer ticks
for the first hour of the kiln's progress
I think about tomorrow
at its opening—lifting out
these bones of a new creation.

A minor touch here,
a movement there
has changed it
birthing new meaning to the work.
A chance to re-vision
what the wet clay had murmured.

This new canvas—
bleached white from the fire
receives paint drips and brushstrokes
along its smooth and textured body.
Complete only when the
colors merge onto its sculpted skin.

MIRRORS

Mirrors, mirrors, on the wall
We created these last fall.
They tell a story of reflection
Like how our words
Make an impression,
Cause a sensation,
Give inspiration,
Illumination,
And motivation.

These mirrors also show and tell
How some of us might see, as well.
We see ourselves in different ways
And it often depends upon the day.
Sometimes we're happy
Sometimes we're sad.
Smart or silly
Even bad.
We're all so different
This is true
When you look at each mirror
You might see something too.

PEACE BY PIECE, WITH LOVE

We thought about peace and love
as we traced our hands in clay.
Shaping fingers
into peace signs
and love signs.
Wishing for peace on earth
in every way.

Our beautiful, sculpted hands
bright with rings on fingers,
and polish on nails,
shout proudly
to love one another, right now.

We've created art
representing a strong, simple gesture
of holding hands high,
with fingers curled,
in the name of love
with hope for peace.

We've been singing
songs of peace.
Chanting our message,
to give peace a chance.

We've heard of peace pipes,
and peace treaties,
and some of us long
to find inner peace.

So . . . peace, everyone.
These hands are our love story.
Peace be with you.
You know she loves you.
Take another little piece of my heart.
And love, love me do.

VOICES

Poems come and go.
Rhythms rise and fall.
A cardinal chirps and trills.
The oriole sputters and chants
melodic song.

We speak in varied tones
on impulse and
experience of the
day,
hour,
minute.
Like the warbler's tune
changes from romance to
flight.
These are voices
all have to share—
speaking words of woe
or songs of grace.

Communication is all
encompassing to life—
growls and shrieks
of dog and fox,
hum of bumble bee flower lovers,
chatter of squirrels
guarding piles of seed,
a hawk's call arousing fear,
"I love you" under the elm.

All speak a language
of sound and syllable.
Conveying feelings, defenses,
love and fear.

Listeners comprehend
the meaning—
each species understood
by their own, yet,
willing to decipher
the unfamiliar.

Speak, sing, tap
and roar,
clap, trill, snarl
and purr,
snort, squeal,
whinny and splash.

En Français

"Bonjour,
comment sa vas,"
we whispered giddily
to the boy scouts
camped in the woods
behind my house.
"Ah, bien, merci,
tout le monde,
oui, mon ami!"
Anything we could
pull out of our
French class memory
we crooned to the
utterly fascinated boys.
They were our age
so, of course, it was
a flirtatious act
defining ourselves
as chic French girls.

Bonnie was the interpreter
explaining to the troop members
that *"ne parle pas anglais."*
Back and forth we strode
around the camp
making an obvious impression.
The boys would ask Bon to
ask me a question
which she did in her
most fluid accent.
I would *"oui"* or *"non"*
or *"merci"* my way out
of being found out.

Oh, what a joy to
play-act on this camp stage.

Years later in college
Bon and I took a summer
French class with a
rather large, slimy professor.

He gave all of us French names.
Babbette and Elise we were christened.
He spoke Babbette in sharp choppy rhythm
Elise was swirled around
his mouth, saliva spewing
as he said Eleeeese
splat!
We were always giggling
in the back row
while he taught the class
playing with the language
as we did for my acting debut
in the woods with Bon and the boy scouts.

First Flight

Felix brought his missus
along with their fledgling
for its first flight.
The little one hopped
awkwardly
as Felix and mom called out
madly.

All the little birds
that nest nearby
came for the occasion.

The redstart
called to the baby
from its perch
in the pear tree.

A young hummingbird
sat on a rosebush branch
to watch the celebration.

Even the comic catbird
landed, to witness his progress.

A chestnut-sided warbler
called out to the baby
as did everyone
to encourage his flight.

Felix and mom
persisted
with their wild song
even with green worms
and white moths
held in their beaks.

SKY BRIDGE

The hawk's whistle
turned my head
to look up
as he floated
alone
in circles
calling—
then gone.

Moments later
my head turned
to gaze aloft
responding to
the call
again.

This time
he and mate
are soaring
so high
they are mere
dark figures
in the big sky—
tracing the arc
of a rainbow
that formed
a bridge
between clouds.

It stayed longer
in the sky
than the hawks
who had called me

to look
then vanished—
their purpose,
fulfilled.

KNOWING

God danced
with me tonight—
twirling me around
and around so fast
I could not see
nor focus
on one thing
as we twirled and swayed
twisted and swirled.

Oh!
I felt so free
and loose
and light
moving silently and
effortlessly
through space.

My movements
guided.
I felt no part in
creating our motion
in this free dance
of reverence.

Twirl me to the right.
Twirl me to the left.
Spin me around and around
till I should drop.
Yet, I am held
to swing once more.

I must ask to dance
more often.
Not wait until
the last minute.
But ask
to be held
in this divine
embrace.
Turn me left
turn me right.
Spin me
around and around.
But pull me back
and hold me
real close
when I get dizzy.

INSTANT SORROW

They were blood brothers so dear
one a lot older and highly revered
by the younger one who wore
love on his sleeve by
following his footsteps and
taking his lead.

A date was planned
for the brothers to meet
by the side of a brook
to go fishing as a treat.
The young one would follow
at the end of the day
after his work he'd drive up
that way to the brook
and his brother without delay.

At the time that they planned
the young one set out but
was stopped by his parents
on the road with a shout
They told of the heartbreak
of an accident up there
by the side of the brook
a fall down through the air
down so hard to the ground
that his death was so fast
this brother so loved now
a memory of the past.

The shock and the loss
the anger and whys
brought an instant sorrow
to so many lives.

And the younger brother
living these many years
still mourns the loss
often with tears.

MEETING LENNY AT BENIHANA

As steel blades spark
and slice on the searing grille
I sit with the father
I never knew until this day—
thirty years a stranger.
Yet, now this man,
whom I resemble so profoundly,
tickles my interest and confusion.

Lenny is a funny man
a sunny man—
joking and invoking
humor and camaraderie
toward all who sit
around us at this
Asian food spectacle
of technique and flavor.

While the carrots spin above
and the steak sizzles
I am kissed and hugged
more in these moments
than in my lifetime of
parenting by the man who raised me.

My jaw drops
and eyes widen
with each thrust
of the knife
and humor from
this stranger—a comedienne
and singer by profession.
Qualities that overlap off stage
to the audience of diners

around us—enthusiastically
exchanging phone numbers—
eager to share another engagement
of wit and friendship.

He is as wild and colorful
as my father was serious
and reserved.
Both traits define me
and I wonder how it
would have been to grow up
in his lively shadow
singing and joking my way
through life.
Would I have been happier
living with a man who
disappeared for months
on his road trips
of glory and recognition
while mother stoked
the flames of home and hearth
love and security?

Questions never to be answered.
Yet, this evening of
food and fun seeps into
my longing bones.

KNOCK ON THE DOOR

In my sorrow
knowing death was nearing
my mother's side
I cried for the first time
that morning feeling
so helpless and
uncomforted by anything
except the days that I still
had before that fateful moment.

Yet, this morning
alone with my fears
and sadness I wept to
the spirit that I yearned for
to help extend
her time on earth.

Please make her well, I insisted.
Let her walk again, I shouted.
Take away her pain, I sobbed.
Let me have her for more time.

What can I do? I questioned.
Is there some hope? I asked.
Can she be healed? I pondered
in my loudest voice
soaked in tears
reaching out of my own way
to the large big force of life
for answers
reassurance . . . anything!

Give me a sign, I said.
Let me know that you hear me
that you are with us
that we are with you
. . . please!
Suddenly, there was a knock on the door.

PICKING BERRIES

Every year we trek to the mountainside
to pick raspberries and blueberries.

Dad is so excited to
land at this destination
rich with succulent fruit.

He jokes with the attendant
about getting weighed
before we start picking
and upon our return.

Once we are situated
amongst the bushes
he teases
while placing berries
in his basket and also in his mouth.
"One for you and one for me,"
he hums.

The clear sky,
birds singing and
happy people
gathered to
pick this bounty
for the jam
and pies they will create
uplifts.

Our labor is rewarded with
an abundance of berries
to take home
for our own jam production.

Certo, jars, and sugar
fill our grocery cart
as we purchase the ingredients
for this process.

Though, we have done this for years
we still carefully read the directions
for this fruity recipe,
each of us taking on
our specific manufacturing roles.

As the fruit bubbles and steam rises
Dad is writing "Leo's Raspberry Jam"
and "Leo's Blueberry Jam" labels.
The final defining moment of this
sweet summer ritual.

LET'S HIT THE ROAD

I want to hit the road,
going to places so distant
from here.
Off to barren mountains
with fir-lined ledges—
desert brightness
capturing the sand.

Lush vineyards bursting
with nectar,
cliffsides over the sea.

I want to wake up to sunbeams,
nestle under the stars at night
in a new place
with a new landscape—
rocky, sandy, spruce or pine.
The elms, oaks, cherry and ash
left behind,
as I discover
how the earth changes her mind.

It is harsh and dry
moist and thick.
Carpeted in green,
eroded and lined.

I want to go to a new place
with a diversity of smells—
jasmine and rose
sage and cedar
saltwater and sand.
I want to taste foods
cooked with spices, rare
aroma and flavor unlike anywhere.

Let's hit the road.
Picnic on our way
with stops for a view
or a walk for the day.
I want to see it all
in a leisurely way.

TREE FIRE

The blue light
of flame
sways to the
rhythm of the
burn.

Orange tongues
lick the charred
wood
warming and scenting
the room.

This inferno clears
the stove's glass window
of soot and resin
so the fire dance
is visible.

There is a comfort
in heat fueled
with maple, cherry
apple and ash.

Once standing to the
heavens
roots tangled in the earth.
Now they give
in death
as they once sheltered
new life
on leafed limb.

CONCERT HURRICANE

A storm of youthful memories
uprooted last night
as each beat and strum
transported us
to the days when
our music was born.

Rockers still in leather
played with wild reverence—
their smiles capturing
each moment of pleasure
the soulful melody inspired.

Generous collaboration
pulsed on the stage.
A wind of diverse voices
sang poetry
beat drums
and guitar chords.
Horn blowers
called rhythms to the crowd
joyfully dancing
to each note.

Uplifted by the
tempest of harmonies
and vibration
we were one with
all who witnessed this
musical wonder
last night.

MAGIC

I believe in magic.
I see it everywhere—
from butterfly metamorphose
to bird migration.
Magical feats
of strength, determination,
patience and crafting.

I see magic
in spider web stringing,
bird nest weaving,
hummingbird hovering,
seedlings pushing
through soil.

I believe in the magic of birth itself—
mothers cradling young
within their bodies or
hatching eggs that
crack with life.

I see magic
in the daily tricks
of dawn and dusk
painting color on the sky.
The deep black
of night splattered
with sparkling light.

Rainbows reaching across
clouds, bridging the horizon.
The scent of flowers in a
burst of bloom.

Bees storing honey in
waxy combs.
The death of fall,
chill of winter white,
music and color
reappearing in spring,
summer's sultry buzz.

The Sun on our Trail

Take a ride with us.
We'll bring you to the sun.
We'll curve around
narrow roadways
toward blue sky
and mountain silhouette
backlit in white,
defining soft peaks,
so distant.

We always find
the sun.
Even on dark days
cloudy and drizzled,
the sky will open,
guiding us in light
through vibrant countryside,
savoring each view
as the day turns.

Later,
on our journey home
the sky darkens
to the somber hue
we had left
hours before.

The sun always
finds us.
Let's go for a ride.

About the Author

Leslie Klein is an artist and writer, living in the Berkshires of Massachusetts.

Her op-eds, feature stories, and poetry have been published in various newspapers and magazines.

Klein has had a long career teaching and showing her work in galleries and juried exhibitions. She was commissioned to create the sculpture for The Boston Freedom Award.

CPSIA information can be obtained
at www.ICGtesting.com
Printed in the USA
BVHW081149220620
582046BV00001BA/64

9 781951 651343